DEDICATION

To all the athletes who have ever stepped onto the basketball
court with passion and determination, this book is for you.
To the coaches who inspire, mentor, and push their players
to greatness.
To the families and friends who support, encourage, and
celebrate the triumphs and setbacks.
And to the countless individuals, who have faced adversity,
overcome self-doubt, and emerged stronger, this book
honors your resilience.
May the insights within these pages fuel your pursuit of
excellence, ignite your inner strength, and remind you that
the greatest victories are often won within.
With gratitude and respect.

iv

BASKETBALL SPORTS PSYCHOLOGY

A sport inspired guide that help improve your basketball game and all aspect of your life through sportsmanship and team spirit for kids and adults.

JACK MICHAEL

TABLE OF CONTENTS

DEDICATION..iii

TABLE OF CONTENTS v

ACKNOWLEDGMENTS i

INTRODUCTION ii

CHAPTER 1..1

JAMES NAISMITH'S BASKETBALL RULES 1

CHAPTER 2...i

THE ESSENTIAL BASKETBALL SKILLS...i

CHAPTER 3..3

ALLOCATE TIME FOR THE FUNDAMENTALS 3

Why Self-Belief is Important in Sports.....................................3

CHAPTER 4..6

BASKETBALL MINDSET TECHNIQUES TO HELP YOU SUCCEED.....................6

Building Your Basketball Mentality 6

Effective Communication: The Heart of Team Dynamics......................11

Emotional Intelligence: The Glue of Strong Teams 12

CHAPTER 5..14

TRUST YOUR COACH AND TEAMMATES..................................14

Keep an Open Mind for Learning 15

Stay Focused During Training 16

Player-Coach Relationships: Effective Communication and Conflict Resolution...18

Conflict Resolution Techniques 19

CHAPTER 6..22

LEAVE YOUR COMFORT ZONE 22

    Keep Training beyond Practice 23

CHAPTER 7 25

IMPROVE YOUR HUMAN CAPACITY 25

    Pre-Game Routine 26

    In-Game Focus 27

    The Prevalence of Mental Health Issues in Basketball 28

    Recognizing Signs and Symptoms of Distress 29

    Role of coaches and team staff 31

    Player-centered approaches to mental health 32

CHAPTER 8 33

PLAY INTENSIVE DEFENSE 33

    The mindset of a defensive warrior 34

CHAPTER 9 37

IDENTIFY YOUR PERSONAL ASSETS AND WEAKNESSES 37

    Competition and Performance Under Pressure 39

CHAPTER 10 44

USE IN-GAME MISTAKES AS LESSON 44

    Three strategies to help you develop confidence 45

CHAPTER 11 47

DEFENSIVE STRATEGIES USED OFTEN 47

    Combination Defenses 52

CONCLUSION 54

ACKNOWLEDGMENTS

I extend my deepest gratitude to the individuals who have contributed to the creation of Basketball Sports Psychology.
To my family, whose unwavering support and patience fueled my passion for this project.
To the sports psychologists, coaches, and athletes who shared their insights and experiences, enrich the book with real-world perspectives.
To the researchers and scholars whose groundbreaking work laid the foundation for this exploration of basketball sports psychology.
Special thanks to:
Coach Jane Doe, whose expertise and enthusiasm inspired countless pages.
The players and teams who graciously shared their stories, struggles, and triumphs.
This book would not have been possible without your collective wisdom, encouragement, and dedication.

INTRODUCTION

Basketball isn't just about physical strength, speed, or shooting accuracy; it's a mind game. **In Basketball Sports Psychology**, we dive deep into the mental strategies that separate great players from legends. Whether you're a player looking to sharpen your focus, boost your confidence, or gain that winning edge, this book will guide you to a new level of play.

The court is a kind of battlefield where mental toughness is just as vital as physical skill. Through understanding your thoughts, emotions, and behaviors, you'll learn how to stay calm under pressure, outsmart your opponents, and lead your team to victory. Discover how elite players prepare mentally for success and how you, too, can master the psychology of basketball to stand out.

This book offers practical techniques that help you perform at your best, no matter the stakes. From managing stress to building a champion's mindset, this guide empowers you to overcome obstacles and win—every time. Take charge of your mental game, and watch your performance reach new heights. Your next victory is just a mindset away.

CHAPTER 1

JAMES NAISMITH'S BASKETBALL RULES

1. You can throw the ball in any direction using one or both hands.

2. The ball may be batted in any direction with one or both hands (never using a fist).

3. Players are not allowed to run while holding the ball. If a player catches the ball while running at a good speed, they must stop and throw the ball from where they caught it.

4. The ball must be held with the hands only; using arms or the body to hold it is not allowed.

5. No player may push, shove, trip, shoulder, or physically harm an opponent in any way. The first violation counts as a foul, and the second disqualifies the player until the next goal is scored. If there's intent to cause harm, the player is out for the rest of

the game with no substitution.

6. Making contact with the ball using a fist, or breaking rules 3, 4, or causing harm as stated in Rule 5, results in a foul.

7. If a team makes three fouls in a row without the other team fouling, the other team gets a goal.

8. A goal is made when the ball is thrown or knocked into the basket and stays in, as long as the defenders don't touch or disturb it.

9. When the ball goes out of bounds, the player who last touched it must throw it back into play. If there's any disagreement, the umpire throws it onto the field. The throw must be made within 5 seconds, or the ball goes to the opposing team. Delaying the game results in a foul.

10. The umpire will keep track of fouls and has the authority to disqualify players based on Rule 5.

11. The referee oversees the ball, decides if it's in play, determines possession, keeps score, and signals when a goal has been scored. They handle all duties expected of a referee.

12. The game is divided into two 15-minute halves, with a 5-minute break between them.

13. The team with the most goals at the end of the game is the winner. If there's a tie, the captains can decide to continue playing until a goal is scored.

CHAPTER 2

THE ESSENTIAL BASKETBALL SKILLS

While many skills contribute to a strong basketball game, only a few should be prioritized in your training plan. Most fundamental skills are connected, so improving one area will naturally enhance others. Focus on mastering one or two of these skills at a time. You'll notice that while you're sharpening specific abilities, other parts of your game will improve too.

Shooting

Shooting is one of the most important skill in basketball game. No matter how well you play, if you can't make shots, winning becomes nearly impossible. Mastering the mechanics—holding, aiming, and releasing the ball under pressure—takes practice. Being shot-ready, balanced, and squared to the basket while maintaining proper form is a key challenge.

4 Essential Elements of Great Shooting:

To develop a solid shot, you'll need consistent practice. Make it your goal to shoot hundreds of shots daily during the off-season, including layups, jump shots, and free throws. The more you commit, the better you'll get.

Passing

Basketball is a team sport, and passing is crucial for setting up plays. While accuracy is important, reacting quickly under defensive pressure is what really counts. Great passers help elevate their teammates, creating opportunities for them to score. They also minimize turnovers, leading to more points and fewer mistakes. Coaches value players who can pass effectively, knowing it benefits the entire team.

Dribbling

Dribbling is a basic skill that every basketball player must have. Without strong dribbling and ball-handling abilities, advancing down the court is nearly impossible. Focused practice on dribbling and ball control every day will result in noticeable improvement over time, allowing you to move the ball fluidly and avoid costly violations.

Footwork

Good footwork is essential in all areas of basketball— whether you're shooting, defending, rebounding, or moving down the court. The way you move your feet will directly impact your ability to execute plays and perform at your best.

Mastering these essential skills will greatly enhance your overall basketball performance, making you a more effective and well-rounded player.

CHAPTER 3

ALLOCATE TIME FOR THE FUNDAMENTALS

Regardless of which role you aim to play or which skills feel natural, dedicating time to sharpen each fundamental is essential. The more you develop your skills, the more complete you become as a player. Most positions in basketball require a variety of skills, and as you work on one area, other parts of your game will naturally improve. These core basketball talents often overlap, so you'll continue to rely on and refine them throughout your career.

If you keep saying, "I can't do it," you're only getting in your own limited way. Instead, focus on the challenge and change your mindset. After all, everyone faces struggles—it's part of being human.

Why Self-Belief is Important in Sports

Believing in yourself is vital in any sport. Imagine giving up just before scoring a goal in football simply because you doubted your ability. In every game, the goal is to score and win, so always give your best effort, even when self-doubt creeps in. Don't allow the fear of failure to stand in the way of your growth and progress. Remember, no one is perfect. In fact, it's likely you'll miss more shots than you make, but that's okay—it's part of the game.

I'm fortunate to have a great physical education teacher, Mr. Wood, at Roman Hill Primary School. Without his support, I wouldn't be as confident as I am today. He taught me the power of self-belief, encouraged me to take on new challenges, and helped me push through self-doubt. Having someone to boost your confidence can make all the difference.

A Lesson in Self-Belief

One particular moment stands out for me—a basketball game where my team made it to the championship. We faced a strong opponent, and the game was intense. I fell down countless times and even got hurt. Mr. Wood kept telling me to take a break, but I refused because I believed I could push through. Even though we didn't win the game, I was incredibly proud of myself and my team for giving it our all.

My Own Belief

Self-confidence is crucial for everyone. When you believe in yourself, you can accomplish anything you aim for. Sure, there will be obstacles, and you might feel like quitting, but if you keep going, success will come.

Confidence isn't just for big moments—it's in the small things too, like completing your homework or cleaning your room. These actions, however small, build self-belief. And showing up for school and learning? That's an investment in your future.

CHAPTER 4

BASKETBALL MINDSET TECHNIQUES TO HELP YOU SUCCEED

Building Your Basketball Mentality

You might already possess the physical abilities, stamina, height, and athleticism needed to excel in basketball. However, without developing the right mindset, you won't be able to take your game to the next level. The skills you learn and the attitude you bring to the court work hand in hand, helping you rise as a successful basketball player.

The Mindset of a Basketball Superstar

To develop a winning mentality, focus on building teamwork and a strong personal spirit. These qualities will help you overcome obstacles and give you the mental toughness to succeed on the court. We'll also highlight the core traits you should foster to thrive under pressure.

Your Personal Spirit

Whether you're practicing solo or with a team, your own inner drive will be key to your success. By nurturing qualities like discipline, resilience, and determination, you'll grow as a player—mentally, emotionally, and physically.

Believe in Yourself

Always trust in your abilities. Perfection isn't the goal—improvement is. Self-doubt will only hold you back. Instead, focus on your strengths and never question your potential.

Learning from Role Models

Great players have learned tough lessons on their path to success. Study their mistakes and achievements, adopt their mental toughness, and apply it to your game. Their mindset has been their key to long-lasting success.

Perseverance and Determination

Persistence and resilience are essential traits for any basketball star. You can spend hours honing your skills, but without the will to outlast your competition, you'll struggle to reach your full potential Stay dedicated and keep pushing forward, even when things get difficult.

Mastering Your Emotions

We all experience emotions, and they can be powerful allies or obstacles on the court. The key is to maintain control over your emotions. Don't let other players, referees, or situations affect your focus. Always remember—you are in control of your thoughts and reactions.

Sharpening Focus and Awareness

Basketball demands intense focus and awareness at all times. It's easy to get distracted, but the best players stay mentally sharp, always aware of their surroundings, both on and off the court.

Confidence without Arrogance

Confidence is the quiet belief in your abilities, reflected in how you play, move, and carry yourself on the court. It's not about arrogance, which often hides insecurity. True confidence empowers you to play your best without needing to show off.

Staying Calm under Pressure

When the game gets intense, and things start to unravel, staying composed is key. Great players thrive under pressure and perform at their best when the stakes are high. Keep a cool head, and your skills will shine through.

Desire to Improve

To become a better player, you must constantly strive to grow. Embrace the challenges, push beyond your comfort zone, and learn from your mistakes. This desire to improve will set you apart from others.

Focus on Solutions, Not Problems

When faced with difficulties, it's easy to dwell on problems. Instead, shift your mindset toward finding solutions. Learn to ask the right questions and think creatively to overcome challenges on the court.

Patience and Discipline

Basketball mastery takes time. Patience and discipline are

very crucial for long term success. Stay committed to your training, keep practicing, and continuously seek out ways to improve.

Decisiveness on the Court

In basketball, hesitation can cost you the game. Be confident in your decisions and act swiftly. Mistakes are part of the learning process, but indecision will hold you back.

Courage and Heart

Basketball is a game of bravery. Playing with heart and pushing yourself beyond your limits will earn the respect of your teammates and the crowd. Courage on the court matters more than skill alone.

Setting Regular Goals

Great players are always setting goals. Either short-term/long-term, these goals will guide your development and keep you well motivated. Setting clear objectives for your basketball growth will keep you on track to success.

The Spirit of Teamwork

Basketball is a team sport. Cultivate a sense of teamwork and build strong connections with your teammates, coaches, and club. Together, you'll achieve greater success on the court.

Team Dynamics: Understanding Group Psychology and Communication

Effective teamwork is essential to success in basketball. When players unite around a shared goal, they create a complex environment shaped by psychological, emotional, and social factors. A strong grasp of team dynamics helps coaches, players, and staffs build a positive, high-performing atmosphere.

The Power of Team Cohesion

A cohesive team is much more than a collection of talented individuals. It's the synergy of diverse skills, perspectives, and experiences working together toward a common purpose. When team members feel connected, valued, and supported, they are more likely to:

- Communicate openly and honestly.
- Trust one another's strengths and limitations.
- Show empathy and understanding.
- Collaborate effectively.
- Overcome challenges with resilience.

Understanding Group Psychology

Team dynamics are deeply influenced by group psychology. Key factors to consider include:

1. Group Norms: These are the unspoken rules that guide team behavior and shape its culture.

2. Social Identity: Each player's sense of belonging and self within the group.

3. Cohesion: The emotional and practical bond that holds the team together, strengthened by shared experiences.

4. Conflict: Disagreements are unavoidable, but they can either strengthen or strain relationships, depending on how they're handled.

5. Leadership: A strong leader inspires the team's culture, direction, and motivation.

Effective Communication: The Heart of Team Dynamics

Good communication is the foundation of a successful team. It:

1. Builds trust: Encourages open dialogue, active listening, and transparency.

2. Prevents misunderstandings: Clarifies roles, expectations, and goals.

3. Resolves conflicts: Tackles problems head-on with respect and understanding.

4. Boosts Morale: Recognizes and celebrates both individual and team achievements.

5. Improves collaboration: Welcomes diverse opinions and fosters idea-sharing.

Key Communication Strategies

Active Listening: Focus on understanding the speaker fully.

Clear Messaging: Be precise and avoid ambiguity.

Non-Verbal Cues: Be very attentive to tone use, body language and facial expressions.

Constructive Feedback: Provide specific, supportive, and actionable feedback.

Regular Team Meetings: Create opportunities for open dialogue, reflection, and planning.

Emotional Intelligence: The Glue of Strong Teams

Emotional intelligence (EI) helps players manage social interactions, control their emotions, and strengthen relationships.

1. Self-Awareness: Recognize your own emotions and how they affect those around you.

2. Empathy: Acknowledge and appreciate the feelings and viewpoints of your teammates.

3. Social Skills: Develop the ability to resolve conflicts and build stronger team relationships.

Building a Positive Team Culture

A strong team culture is fostered through:

1. Shared Values: Create a clear team identity rooted in common goals.

2. Inclusivity: Make sure everyone feels they belong and are appreciated.

3. Supportive Leadership: Encourage personal growth and well-being.

4. Celebrating Successes: Acknowledge individual and

team wins, big or small.

5. Learning from Failures: Treat setbacks as opportunities to improve.

Unlocking Your Team's Potential

Team dynamics are shaped by psychological, emotional, and social factors. By understanding group psychology, encouraging open communication, and developing emotional intelligence, your team can unlock its full potential. Remember, a united and cohesive team is far greater than the sum of its individual players.

Note:

1. Set up clear channels for communication and outline expectations.

2. Build a positive team culture rooted in shared values and inclusivity.

3. Develop emotional intelligence by focusing on self-awareness, empathy, and social skills.

4. Practice active listening, offer constructive feedback, and hold regular team discussions.

5. Acknowledge and celebrate both individual and team achievements.

By incorporating these strategies, you'll build a stronger, more unified team that thrives both on and off the court.

CHAPTER 5

TRUST YOUR COACH AND TEAMMATES

When others trust us, it sparks a drive within to achieve even greater success. That's why it's so important to openly support your teammates and coach. Having even a small amount of faith in someone can create a huge impact. Interestingly, the belief you show in others often circles back, boosting your morale and strengthening the team bond.

Build Friendships

The people we trust and enjoy playing with the most are often our closest friends. If you don't know your teammates well, take the time to connect with them. Ask about their families, interests, and hobbies. Finding common ground helps create strong bonds, making you feel more united on and off the court.

Show Commitment

Commitment is not just about attending practices. Stay late, work on your game, and help teammates struggling with certain aspects of theirs. These actions show that you're fully dedicated to the team's success and growth.

Foster Cooperation

When everyone on the team is working toward a shared goal, something magical happens—it's called synergy. Synergy is when the group becomes stronger than the sum of its parts, and that's only possible when there's genuine cooperation. Be the first to extend a hand and help build this collective effort.

Bring Enthusiasm

Passion and excitement are contagious. When you bring energy and enthusiasm to the game, you uplift the entire team Basketball is just as much a mental game as a physical one, and a positive mindset can provide your team with the boost they need to tackle challenges and stay motivated.

Stay Loyal

Imagine loyalty as the steadfast devotion of a dog—no matter what happens, it remains constant, their loyalty remains intact. Build that same sense of loyalty among your team. Support your teammates through the highs and lows, and always have their backs. This loyalty will help build a culture of trust and unity within the team.

Keep an Open Mind for Learning

To grow as a player, you must remain eager to learn and improve. Basketball, like life, is all about learning and adapting. How you handle yourself on the court often mirrors how you navigate life. By staying open to learning from your experiences in both basketball and life, you'll grow not just as a player, but as a person.

What to avoid

Stop Making Excuses

Excuses will only hold you back. No one wants to hear why you didn't perform well or what went wrong with the game. Excuses are for those who aren't willing to grow. If you want to improve, take responsibility for your actions and leave excuses behind.

Control Your Emotions

Losing emotional control during a game can throw off your decision-making and impact your performance. When you react emotionally, you lose focus and start to spiral. Maintain emotional discipline so that your intelligence and skills guide you, not your emotions.

Don't Blame Your Teammates

Basketball is a team effort. When things don't turn out the way you expected, try not to point fingers at others. Pointing fingers only creates division, and ultimately, the team wins or loses together. Use challenges as chances to learn and grow, rather than criticize or undermine one another. Don't Fear Mistakes

Basketball is full of mistakes, and that's okay. Every mistake you make is an opportunity to learn, grow, and improve for the next game. Embrace your errors—they are stepping stones on the journey to success.

Stay Focused During Training
Your daily training is where true growth happens. What you

do in practice, before, during, and after, directly shapes the player you become. Here's what to keep in mind:

Commit to Your Training

To excel, you need an unwavering commitment. Show dedication by being punctual, participating fully, and pushing yourself to improve.

Arrive Early and Stay Late

Being the first to arrive and the last to leave sends a strong message about your commitment. Use this extra time to sharpen your skills, talk to your coach, or focus on building endurance and proficiency.

Take Initiative in Drills

Get involved in drills and activities right away. Active participation leads to growth. Don't shy away from making mistakes—everyone is a chance to learn something new.

Ask Insightful Questions

Show your coach and teammates that you're engaged by asking thoughtful questions that challenge the team's strategies and encourage new ideas.

Give Your All in Drills

Drills are the foundation of every player's skillset. Participate fully and push yourself to get the most out of each exercise. It's in these moments that you refine your abilities and improve your game.

Player-Coach Relationships: Effective Communication and Conflict Resolution

The player-coach relationship is a vital component of success in basketball. This dynamic partnership requires mutual respect, trust, and effective communication to foster growth, development, and peak performance. When coaches and players connect on a personal and professional level, they create a powerful synergy that drives team success.

Understanding the Emotional Connection

Player-coach relationships involve complex emotions, influencing interactions and outcomes. Coaches need to be very much aware and manage their own emotions and those of their players. Emotional intelligence helps coaches:

- Understand player motivations and concerns
- Empathize with player struggles and frustrations
- Develop personalized communication strategies
- Foster trust by practicing active listening and showing empathy.

Effective Communication Strategies

Good communication is the basic of successful player coach relationships. Coaches should:

- Use straightforward language, avoiding ambiguity Listen actively, focusing on player concerns
- Provide constructive feedback, balancing criticism with encouragement
- Foster open dialogue, encouraging players to express thoughts and feelings
- Address conflicts promptly, resolving issues before they escalate

Conflict Resolution Techniques

Conflicts inevitably arise in player-coach relationships. Effective conflict resolution requires:

- Remaining calm and composed under pressure
- Identifying underlying issues and concerns
- Addressing conflicts directly, avoiding passive-aggressive behavior
- Seeking common ground and mutually beneficial solutions
- Maintaining respect and professionalism throughout the process

The Power of Empathy and Active Listening

Empathy and active listening are key elements of effective communication.

By truly understanding player perspectives, coaches:

- Build trust and rapport
- Foster a supportive team environment
- Enhance player confidence and motivation
- Resolve conflicts more efficiently

Player-Centered Communication

Player-centered communication prioritizes individual needs and concerns. Coaches should:

- Understand player goals, values, and motivations
- Tailor communication to individual learning styles
- Provide regular feedback and encouragement
- Involve players in decision-making processes

Cultural Sensitivity and Diversity Awareness

Coaches must recognize and respect cultural differences, adapting communication strategies to meet diverse needs. This includes:

- Understanding cultural nuances and values
- Avoiding stereotypes and biases
- Fostering an inclusive team environment
- Addressing cultural conflicts sensitively

Long-Term Relationship Building

Player-coach relationships extend beyond the playing career. Coaches should:

- Invest in players' personal growth and development
- Maintain relationships post-graduation or retirement
- Provide guidance and mentorship throughout life transitions

Challenges and Opportunities

Player-coach relationships face challenges, such as:

- Generational differences and communication gaps
- Conflicting personalities and values
- External pressures and expectations

However, these challenges also present opportunities for growth, learning, and relationship strengthening.

Best Practices for Coaches

To cultivate effective player-coach relationships:

- Prioritize communication and empathy
- Foster a positive team culture
- Address conflicts promptly and professionally

- Seek feedback from players and peers
- Continuously develop emotional intelligence and coaching skills

Finally, the player-coach relationship is a complex, emotionally charged dynamic that demands effective communication, empathy, and conflict resolution. By investing in this relationship, coaches and players can build trust, foster growth, and achieve success on and off the court.

Also Note:

- Develop emotional intelligence to better understand player motivations and concerns.
- Prioritize open, honest communication to build trust and resolve conflicts.
- Adapt communication strategies to meet individual player needs.
- Cultivate a positive team environment that encourages inclusivity and mutual respect.
- Continuously seek feedback and opportunities for growth.

CHAPTER 6

LEAVE YOUR COMFORT ZONE

Training is all about pushing yourself beyond your limits and honing your skills through consistent effort. During practice, it's your chance to sharpen your abilities so that when game day arrives, you're ready to perform at your best. If you hold back or stay within your comfort zone during training, you'll find it harder to grow as a player and play confidently during games. The question is: Are you using your training time to its fullest potential? Or are you just going through the motions, hoping things will magically improve?

Game Speed Training

To bring the right intensity to the court on game day, you need to train like it's a real game. You have to recreate the pace, pressure, and intensity of an actual match during every drill. By practicing at game speed, both physically and mentally, you'll be prepared to perform when it really matters.

Train with Complete Dedication and Tenacity

Approach every practice session with the same seriousness as you would for the biggest game of the season. The focus and grit you bring to these sessions will reflect in your performance when it counts most.

Don't Be Afraid to Ask for Help

No one will know you need guidance if you don't speak up. Staying silent may give others the impression that you're not fully committed, which could slow your progress. Asking questions and seeking help from your coach or teammates shows that you care about improving and growing. Those who ask are the ones who learn, so never hesitate to ask for advice to boost your basketball IQ and skills.

Keep Training beyond Practice

If you're serious about improving, your training doesn't stop when team practice ends. Here's how you can keep growing outside of official sessions:

Sharpen Your Basketball Skills Daily

To become a standout player, you need to work on your skills every single day. After team practice or when you have some downtime, focus on the fundamentals. For instance, while watching TV, dribble the ball back and forth between your hands as fast as you can. Small exercises like this, done consistently, can have a huge impact on your ball-handling skills. It's just one of many ways you can keep improving.

Visualize Yourself Playing Basketball

Research suggests that visualizing can greatly improve performance. Spend time imagining yourself practicing important skills like shooting, dribbling, and passing. Close your eyes and imagine yourself in a high-pressure moment, like taking a last-second shot, feeling the sounds, sights, and even the emotions of the crowd. The more vividly you visualize, the more you'll see the benefits over time.

Exercise Your Mental Strength

Build strategies that will help you stay mentally tough during games. The way you handle stress on the court mirrors how you handle challenges in daily life. Cultivate mental resilience by applying lessons from basketball to everything you do.

Renew Your Physical Fitness

Basketball demands not just skill but also strength, agility, and endurance. Playing games alone won't develop these traits to their fullest. You need a well-rounded fitness routine to enhance your athleticism and ensure you can keep up with the pace and demands of the game.

CHAPTER 7

IMPROVE YOUR HUMAN CAPACITY

Flexibility

Being flexible will help you move smoothly and with greater agility on the court. Stretching, yoga, Pilates, and similar exercises can help you enhance this critical skill, making you more adaptable in the game.

Strength

Strength is crucial for defending yourself against aggressive plays and minimizing the risk of injury. You can build strength through weightlifting, stair climbing, and engaging in physically challenging tasks.

Endurance

Endurance will keep you going strong when others are worn out, especially in the final moments of the game. You can boost your stamina by incorporating activities like swimming, cycling, walking, and jump roping into your routine. Varying your activities throughout the day will elevate your conditioning and turn you into a player with serious staying power.

Athletics

Improving your athleticism will enhance your ability to jump higher, grab more rebounds, and outmaneuver opponents for shots. Exercises like skipping, stretching, and stair climbing can improve your overall athletic performance. Increased flexibility also plays a big role in becoming a more powerful athlete.

Speed

Speed will help you intercept passes, react quickly on defense, and outpace your opponents on the fast break. You can boost your speed by strengthening your legs, improving your running technique, and practicing sprints. Quick, sharp movements will also improve your ability to change direction rapidly on the court.

Game Day Mindset

To excel on game day, you need to focus, stay sharp, and tap into your competitive drive. Here are a few habits to adopt before, during, and after the game to elevate your performance.

Pre-Game Routine
Listen to Inspirational Music

Music has the power to uplift and energize. Whether it's something upbeat that gets you pumped or a calmer tune that helps you center yourself, take a few minutes before the game to listen to music that puts you in the right mindset. Visualize Success on the Court

As you listen to your pre-game music, take a moment to mentally walk through the game. Imagine making your shots and playing with precision. Visualization can be a powerful tool to sharpen your focus and improve performance.

Stretch Properly

Make sure to stretch your arms, shoulders, neck, and back before stepping onto the court. This will help relax your body and reduce the risk of injuries. Progressive Warm-up at Game Speed

The energy you bring to warm-ups sets the tone for how you'll perform when the game starts. Make sure your warm-up is at game speed to ensure your muscles are ready to go.

In-Game Focus

Communicate with Passion

Communication on the court is essential. Talk to your teammates on both ends of the floor, but make sure your words are meaningful. Use your voice to empower and motivate those around you. When you're on the bench, stand up, support your teammates, and cheer them on with enthusiasm.

Box-Out and Rebound with Determination

When a shot goes up, get into position and aggressively box out your opponent, whether on offense or defense. Once you've cleared space, go after the rebound with full determination.

Share the Ball

No one enjoys playing with someone who hogs the ball. Basketball is a team game, and when you pass the ball around, everyone gets involved. Your teammates will appreciate it and gain confidence, which ultimately boosts your team's chances of success.

Mental Health in Basketball: Recognizing Signs and Symptoms of Distress

Basketball players, like athletes in any high-pressure sport, face numerous physical and emotional demands. While physical health is often the main focus, mental well-being is just as critical. Understanding and addressing mental health challenges in basketball is essential for both performance and overall quality of life.

The Prevalence of Mental Health Issues in Basketball

Mental health struggles can affect players at any level, from local youth leagues to elite professional teams. Some of the basic issues include:

Anxiety and Stress: Related to game performance, competition, and public scrutiny.

Depression and Loneliness: Especially common during periods of injury or extended bench time.

Body Image Concerns: Pressure to maintain peak physical condition can lead to eating disorders or unhealthy habits.

Substance Abuse: Used as a coping mechanism to deal with stress, pain, or mental health struggles.

Trauma and Grief: Stemming from personal experiences, such as family loss, or career-related stress.

Recognizing Signs and Symptoms of Distress

It's important for coaches, teammates, and staff to recognize potential indicators of mental health issues. Some of the warning signs include:

Changes in Appetite or Sleep Patterns: Increased or decreased eating, insomnia, or oversleeping.

Irritability, Mood Swings, or Emotional Outbursts: Sudden shifts in mood or being easily upset.

Withdrawal from Social Interactions: Isolation from teammates, avoiding practices, or skipping social activities.

Decreased Focus or Motivation: Lack of interest in games or practice, decreased performance, or difficulty concentrating.

Physical Complaints Without Medical Causes: Headaches, stomach issues, or other symptoms with no clear physical explanation.

The Effect of Mental Health on Performance

Mental well-being and athletic performance are closely connected. When mental health declines, it can negatively impact several areas, such as:

Decreased Focus and Concentration: Difficulty staying attentive during games or practices.

Slower Reaction Time: Hesitation or delayed decision-making on the court.

Increased Errors: More mistakes during gameplay, potentially costing the team points or wins.

Poor Team Communication: Mental health issues can isolate a player, leading to reduced teamwork and collaboration.

Common barriers to seeking help

Despite the significant impact on performance, many players hesitate to seek help for mental health issues due to:

Stigma: Mental health is often misunderstood, and many fear being labeled as weak or incapable.

Fear of Vulnerability: Athletes often worry that admitting to mental health challenges could harm their reputation or make them seem weak.

Lack of Awareness: Many are unaware of available resources or don't know how to access professional help.

Privacy Concerns: Players may worry that seeking help will not remain confidential, especially in high-profile environments.

Dismantling Obstacles: Building a supportive Environment

To ensure players feel comfortable addressing mental health, it's crucial to create a culture that encourages openness. Key strategies include:

Encouraging Open Discussions: Normalize conversations about mental health in locker rooms, team meetings, and one-on-one talks.

Providing Access to Professional Support: Make licensed therapists, counselors, and mental health professionals easily available to players.

Promoting Self-Care: Incorporate stress management, mindfulness, and relaxation techniques into training routines.

Fostering Empathy: Create a team environment where emotional well-being is taken seriously, and support is readily offered.

Role of coaches and team staff

Coaches and support staff are in a unique position to positively influence players' mental health. Their responsibilities include:

Monitoring Well-Being: Keep an eye on behavioral and emotional changes in players.

Maintaining Communication: Establish an open line of communication so players feel comfortable discussing their issues.

Providing Referrals: Guide players to appropriate mental health resources when necessary.

Modeling Healthy Behaviors: Demonstrate healthy coping mechanisms, self-care habits, and stress management techniques.

Player-centered approaches to mental health

Players can take charge of their mental well-being by:

Seeking Help: Connect with trusted friends, family members, or mental health professionals for support.

Practicing Self-Compassion: Be kind to yourself and recognize the importance of mental wellness.

Engaging in Stress-Reducing Activities: Practice mindfulness, meditation, or participate in hobbies that provide relaxation.

Setting Realistic Expectations: Balance the drive to succeed with a healthy mindset about goals and limitations.

By recognizing the signs of distress and creating an environment that values mental health, basketball teams can ensure both emotional well-being and athletic success.

CHAPTER 8

PLAY INTENSIVE DEFENSE

Learn the foundations of playing a strong, effective defense. Although your shooting will occasionally let you down, your defensive zeal shouldn't, regardless of how ineffective you are on the attacking end of the court.

Strike hardly for loose balls

Players who aggressively compete for the basketball and go to any lengths to win it for their team are adored by coaches. This is an indication of a dedicated, focused player that is regarded and idolized by their teammates and supporters.

Avoid turning over the ball

Basketball is a game where making as few mistakes as possible is crucial. The basketball court is a place where mistakes are absolutely acceptable. To lessen their potential long-term impact on the game, we must quickly take the lessons we can from them. That is, of course, how we develop as players and advances our abilities over time.

Keeping this information in mind, be careful with the ball,

passing it to your teammates with accuracy and care, and refraining from dribbling when a short pass would be a better course of action.

The mindset of a defensive warrior

Playing intensive defense requires a unique mindset, one that combines physical toughness, mental focus, and emotional resilience. It's about embracing the challenge of shutting down opponents, protecting your team's basket, and fueling your squad's momentum.

Understanding the importance of defense

Defense is the foundation of all successful basketball team. It's the difference between winning and losing, between championship glory and playoff disappointment. When you commit to playing intensive defense, you:

- Protect your team's lead and momentum
- Create turnovers and scoring opportunities
- Disrupt opponents' rhythm and confidence
- Build trust and camaraderie with teammates

Key principles of intensive defense

To play intensive defense, focus on these essential principles:

Stay low and balanced: Maintain a defensive stance that allows quick reactions and agile movements.

Be active, not reactive: Anticipate opponents' moves, rather than simply responding.

Keep your head on a swivel: Stay aware of your surroundings, tracking the ball and opponents.

Use your feet, not your hands: Use quick footwork to keep yourself in front of your opponents.

Play help defense: Support teammates by rotating and contesting shots.

The art of defensive positioning: Defensive positioning is crucial to intensive defense. Focus on:

Forcing opponents to their weak side: Limit opponents' scoring options by forcing them to their weaker hand.

Protecting the paint: Defend the basket with determination and authority.

Guarding the perimeter: Harass opponents beyond the three-point line.

The role of communication in intensive defense: Effective communication is vital to intensive defense:

Call out screens and switches: Alert teammates to potential threats.

Provide help and support: Communicate with teammates to ensure seamless rotations.

Celebrate defensive stops: Reinforce positive defensive plays to boost team morale.

Overcoming mental and physical fatigue: Intensive defense demands mental and physical resilience:

Stay focused through adversity: Maintain concentration despite exhaustion or frustration.

Draw energy from teammates: Feed off teammates' enthusiasm and support.

Playing intensive defense requires a unique blend of physical skill, mental toughness, and emotional resilience. By adopting these principles and strategies, you'll turn into a defensive powerhouse.

Note:

- Develop a defensive mindset that fuels your team's success.
- Master key defensive principles, such as staying low and balanced.
- Improve your defensive positioning to protect the paint and perimeter.
- Enhance communication skills to support teammates.
- Overcome mental and physical fatigue through focus and teamwork.

CHAPTER 9

IDENTIFY YOUR PERSONAL ASSETS AND WEAKNESSES

It is crucial to regularly analyze your own and your team's strengths and weaknesses throughout the game in order to adjust your game strategy in a way that will maximize your strengths and minimize your shortcomings. There are essentially a plethora of questions you might ask yourself. But to get you going, here are just a few:

1. How can I use my advantages to the most in this game?

2. How can I play this game while minimizing my weaknesses?

3. In terms of passing, shooting, dribbling, rebounding, handling pressure, etc., what are my teammate's strengths?

4. What are the flaws in my teammate's passing, shooting, dribbling, rebounding, pressure-handling, etc.?

5. How can I make the most of each of my teammate's advantages throughout this game?

6. How can I minimize the flaws of my teammates during this game?

7. What can I do to encourage my teammates to play the game more actively?

Change your game in accordance

You should have enough knowledge and awareness of yourself, your team, and your opponent after responding to all the questions above to be able to modify your game plan accordingly and increase your chances of succeeding. If you don't yet know the answers, it's likely because you haven't asked the correct questions.

Your post-game activities

Most players either wilt in the sadness of failure or bask in the glory of triumph when the game is over. In some ways, it is a very dangerous place to live, even while winning a game is fantastic for team spirit and morale. When we succeed, we usually enjoy ourselves and grow complacent. But when we lose, we reflect, and this is what helps us improve and become a better basketball player.

Learning experiences to identify

Whether you won or lost, every game has the seeds of wisdom that will provide opportunities for you to develop and become a better basketball player.

Take advantage of team strategy and tactics

Consider what went well and poorly for your squad when playing against particular defensive and offensive sets. Also note the times when your team played with the most fervor and the times when you found it difficult to maintain your composure.

Learn from projected personal attitude

Consider the personal attitude you displayed during the game. Consider the questions you asked yourself repeatedly, the thoughts that crossed your mind, and the feelings that swept through your heart. Did they concentrate on issues or solutions? Reflect and give them some serious thought. When you step onto the basketball court for your next game, you will become a better and more effective player the more awareness you gain of your own feelings, questions, and thoughts.

Competition and Performance Under Pressure

Competition fuels sports, motivating athletes to improve and achieve greater success. However, the pressure to perform can become overwhelming, impacting both mental and physical well-being. Recognizing and addressing this pressure is key to thriving in high-stakes environments.

The psychology of competition

In sports, competition is a constant. While it motivates athletes to perform their best, the pressure that comes with it can affect their emotional, mental, and physical health. It's crucial to understand how competition pressure works and how to handle it effectively.

Understanding pressure and its effects

Pressure is the intense stress that athletes feel in competitive situations. It can manifest in various forms:

Physiological: Rapid heart rate, sweating, tight muscles

Emotional: Feelings of anxiety, fear, or doubt

Cognitive: Difficulty focusing, poor decision-making, loss of confidence

Managing pressure and performance

Athletes who excel under pressure are the ones who learn how to manage stress and stay focused.

Here are strategies to help manage that pressure:

Pre-competition preparation

- Create a routine to ease your nerves and keep your mind sharp.
- Visualize yourself succeeding and creating positive outcomes.
- Set goals that are realistic and achievable, avoiding perfectionism.

During competition

- Stay focused on your performance, rather than the result.
- Be mindful of the present moment, shutting out any distractions.

Use positive self-talk to boost your confidence and stay calm.

Post-competition

- Review your performance objectively, looking for areas of improvement.
- Reframe mistakes as learning opportunities instead of failures.
- Keep a mindset that welcomes challenges as a way to grow.

Building resilience under pressure

Resilience is essential for athletes facing high-pressure moments. Building mental and emotional strength helps them stay grounded when the stakes are high.

Developing a growth mindset

- See challenges as chances to grow, not as dangers to avoid.
- Treat failures as lessons for improvement, not as lasting setbacks.

Cultivating self-awareness

- Pay attention to your emotional and physical reactions to pressure.

- Develop techniques to handle stress, such as breathing exercises or mindfulness.

Fostering social support

- Surround yourself with people who lift you up and support your goals.
- Don't hesitate to reach out to coaches, teammates, or mentors for advice and encouragement.

The role of coaches and team staff

Coaches and staff play a key part in helping athletes handle pressure. Their guidance and support can make all the difference during challenging times.

Providing emotional support

- Promote open discussions about the mental side of competition.
- Build a positive and trusting team culture that fosters emotional well-being.

Offering technical guidance

- Help athletes refine their skills and strategies for managing pressure.
- Focus on improving technical aspects of their game to boost confidence.

Creating a supportive environment

- Promote teamwork and build a sense of unity among players.

Foster a mindset of growth and learning among the team.

Also note that, performing under pressure is more than just physical ability—it requires mental toughness and emotional resilience. By understanding competition psychology, managing pressure, building resilience, and fostering a supportive environment, athletes can rise to the challenge and perform at their best.

Note:

- Create a pre-competition routine to help manage stress and focus.
- Stay mindful and grounded during competition to stay sharp.
- Build self-awareness and resilience to handle the pressures of competition.
- Lean on social support and foster a positive team environment.
- Seek guidance and feedback from coaches, mentors, and peers to continuously improve.

These steps can help athletes manage pressure more effectively and perform at their peak in any competitive situation.

CHAPTER 10

USE IN-GAME MISTAKES AS LESSON

Think back to the missed shoots, poor defensive plays, errant passes, other turnovers, etc. You gave your all during the game. Why did these errors happen? And how can you be sure they won't happen again in your subsequent game? Meditate and give it some thought. There are times when the most obvious solutions are not the ones you need. And other times, the simplest solutions will provide you the deepest insights.

Finally, consider all the great things you did during the game. Consider the deft shoots you made, the superb passes you provided to your teammates, the outstanding defensive stops you forced, etc. All you were doing was that. How did you manage this? Can you repeat that during your upcoming game on the basketball court? Meditate and give it some thought.

Three strategies to help you develop confidence

1. If at all feasible, pick a supportive setting, especially when learning a new skill. Not every environment is the same. The optimal atmosphere for growth is one where you are allowed the freedom to make mistakes, kind criticism, and the bravery to go forward. In spite of the ferocious winds and terrible weather, it is possible to exist in Antarctica, but few manage it. In an atmosphere of criticism, perfectionism, and/or insult, confidence also struggles to last. A culture where athletes are respected. When confidence hasn't solidified, a supportive environment is extremely important.

2. Exercise, exercise, exercise! The truly self-assured person enjoys hard work and is prepared to put in the time and effort required to achieve greatness. The distinction between a confident and cocky individual is that the former is capable of acknowledging, discussing, and improving upon his or her shortcomings. You don't let mistakes break you when you have constant confidence. You can develop, learn, and even appreciate mistakes since they help you see where you can get better.

3. Not every thought is the same. Permanent confidence prevents some notions from spending any time in one's

mind. At the door of the mind, thoughts of resentment, self-pity, condemnation, or grandiosity are met. They are not allowed entry if they are destructive thoughts. Genuinely self-assured people are aware that we all have the option to think something or toss it out.

CHAPTER 11
DEFENSIVE STRATEGIES USED OFTEN

Essentially, the goal of a defense is to force the attack to comply with your wishes rather than allowing them to impose their will on you.

Defense requires intelligence, and that intelligence begins with sassing out the many schemes that a team may employ.

While a team may use a variety of defensive tactics during a match, they all eventually fall into one of three categories: man-to-man defense, zone defense, or a combination defense. Each has its advantages and disadvantages, but when used effectively, they can all result in a strong defensive display and perhaps another victory on the court.

Man to man defense

Players are paired with opponents based on position, skill, or stature in this aggressive style of defense, making it easy to spot. When playing man to man, as the name implies, your main objective as a defender is to guard and defend your designated opponent.

You can't really execute other defensive schemes efficiently until you can run man to man coverage and comprehend its principles; you must master man to man play if you want to continue playing at a high level.

Man to man coverage is a great tactic to use when you are evenly matched with an opponent in terms of size, speed, or skill set, according to Rivers. This tactic, often referred to as person-to-person defense, can be implemented in several different ways. The first option is for defenders to play tight man-to-man defense, staying close to their opponent and applying aggressive pressure with minimal space between them. As opposed to close range guarding, a loose man to man defense allows for space between a defender and the ball.

According to Rivers, players who are known to drive aggressively toward the basket and weaker outside shooters often respond well to loose man to man (or sagging man to man) defenses. When there is enough space between a defender and the ball, your defense can stop penetration attempts successfully, if your opponent starts to makes outside shots, it could leave your team vulnerable.

The skill of switching is the last component of the man to man defense. This maneuver is a direct reaction to an offensive screen attempt made in the hopes of relieving pressure for a simpler shot or layup. In man to man combat, players switch offensive opponents rather than attempting to follow and stay with them through a screen. With this switch, there is less likelihood that the offense will be exposed for a driving maneuver or pull-up shot.

You can also use a hedge screen, in which case your big man would come up and take up the space, giving you ample time to pass it and have them get back on their man.

Actually, it's up to the coaches to decide how you should guard the screen.

Zone defense

In zone defensive strategy, you guard a certain region rather than being paired with a specific player like in man to man defense. Zone defenses can be successful against players who are skilled at driving to the basket as well as weak outside shooters. Defenders should pick up opponents as they enter the zone where they are playing defense. Instead of following a player like you would in man to man defense, the defenders hang back and guard their location until they depart or motion to another area of the floor.

The alignments of zone defenses, which are typically

identified by numbers, are broken down.

Typical zone arrangements include:

2-3 zone

The most typical zone layout is this one. The other three defenders guard the baseline, while two players position themselves higher up at the free throw line. Also, stopping baseline and corner attacks, this zone defense is good at grabbing rebounds.

3-2 zone

With three defenders positioned at the free throw line and extra pressure from the wings due to this setup, long-range shots become harder to execute.

1-3-1 zone

One player is positioned above the free throw line, three players are spread throughout the paint, and one player is in charge of guarding the baseline under the basket. This defense is effective at stopping head-on assaults at the top of the circle and driving offenses into awkward positions where they may fall victim to traps or turnovers.

2-1-2 zone

One player is situated in the lane, two other defenders are near the baseline, and two players protect the free throw line.

One man defends above the foul line, and two players defend the wings, the 1-2-2 zone, often known as the jug defense. The baseline is the full responsibility of the last two defenders.

Match-up zone

In a sense, the zone defense plan is a response to the offense's assault. Match-up zone, sometimes referred to as amoeba defense, and is typically deployed from a 2-3 or 1-3-1 beginning alignment before adjusting to the offense's set-up. This tactic is excellent for providing offenses with a genuine match, prompting corner traps, and leading to turnovers. Be careful, though, since offenses that use evasive ways and tactics can win the matchup.

Composite defense

A few alignments create hybrid defense plans by combining man to man and zone defense tactics. These combination defenses can be deployed when you want to change the momentum of the game, start forcing turnovers, etc. When you have defenders who are knowledgeable about man to man concepts and quick enough to recover if and when something goes wrong in coverage, you utilize these defenses.

However, many coaches do not opt for combination

defenses as their default plan due to its mixed approaches.

Combination Defenses
One and Box

This is one of the most popular used defensive strategies. In this setup, one player—often tasked with guarding the opposing team's star or the player on a scoring streak—focuses on that individual. The rest of the defense forms a box shape in the paint, effectively controlling the area and helping to limit inside scoring.

Diamond and One

This strategy is similar to the box-and-one but shifts the formation to a diamond shape. In this arrangement, one defender stays at the foul line while another covers the baseline, with the remaining defenders positioned to effectively guard the perimeter and maintain a solid defensive structure.

Triangle and Two

The triangle-and-two defense is a smart approach when facing a team with two standout players who can dominate the offense. Here, three defenders form a triangle in the paint to prevent easy drives, while the other two players match up in a man-to-man defense against the opposing stars.

Defensive Adjustments

Now that you're familiar with these defensive setups, consider simple adjustments to enhance your team's ability to neutralize the opposing offense. Full-court pressure is one effective tactic, where defenders apply pressure all the way from the baseline to the other end. This method works best with man-to-man defense. Additionally, double-teaming is an option where a second defender assists in guarding a key opponent; although this could leave someone else open for a shot.

Remember, your defensive strategies aren't set in stone. Be prepared to tweak your alignments and tactics throughout the game, as opponents will adjust to your plans. Stay alert, keep these tips in mind, and solidify your presence on the court.

CONCLUSION

Basketball is a game focused on scoring points by getting the ball through a hoop. Played on a rectangular court, points vary based on where the ball is successfully shot. Players can either pass or dribble the ball to advance it. The team with the greatest score at the end of the game wins.

Each team consists of 12 players, but only 5 can be on the court at any given time. The different positions include point guard, shooting guard, center, and forwards (both offensive and defensive). Players can move freely but must establish their positions effectively.

Scoring can happen in three primary ways. A field goal made from beyond the three-point line is worth three points, while shots taken inside that arc usually score two points. The Free throws, awarded for certain fouls, are worth one point each.

A basket made from beyond the three-point line scores three points, while a basket made within the three-point arc earns two points. Each successful free throw is worth one point, and the number of free throws awarded depends on the location of the foul.

Basketball games are won by outscoring your opponents within the allotted time. If the scores are tied at the end, an additional quarter is played to determine the winner.

Printed in Great Britain
by Amazon

48147575R00040